Book 1
Early Elementary

Famous & Fun Jewish Songs

11 Appealing Piano Arrangements

Carol Matz

Famous & Fun Jewish Songs, Book 1, is filled with well-known, beloved Hebrew melodies. The collection contains songs for various Jewish holidays, plus Israeli and Yiddish folk songs, as well as treasured traditional pieces. All of the arrangements are playable within the first few months of piano instruction, and can be used as a supplement to any method. No eighth notes or dotted-quarter rhythms are used. The optional duet parts for teacher or parent add to the fun!

Carol Matz

This series is dedicated to Cantor Irving Shulkes for his warm humor and patient teaching and to my cousin Glenn Dynner, a brilliant author and scholar of Jewish history.

Alfred Music
P.O. Box 10003
Van Nuys, CA 91410-0003
alfred.com

Copyright © 2015 by Alfred Music
All rights reserved. Printed in USA.

No part of this book shall be reproduced, arranged, adapted, recorded, publicly performed, stored in a retrieval system, or transmitted by any means without written permission from the publisher. In order to comply with copyright laws, please apply for such written permission and/or license by contacting the publisher at alfred.com/permissions.

ISBN-10: 1-4706-2962-3
ISBN-13: 978-1-4706-2962-5

Chanukah

Traditional
Arranged by Carol Matz

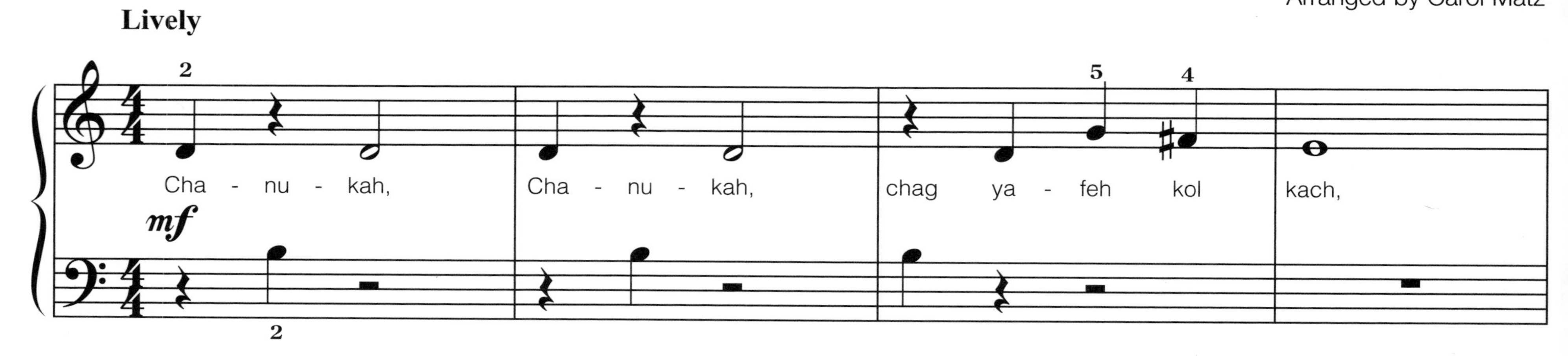

DUET PART (Student plays one octave higher)

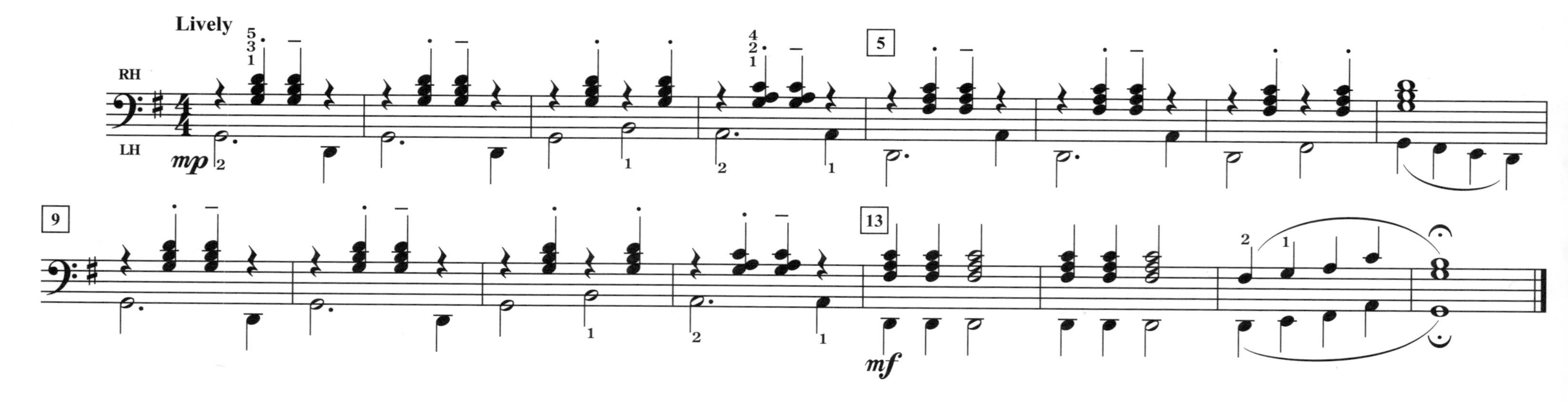

5
1
4
or cha - viv
mi - sa viv,
gil l' - ye - led
rach.
3
9
2
5
4
Cha - nu - kah,
Cha - nu - kah,
s' - vi - von sov,
sov,
2
13
4
sov, sov, sov,
sov, sov, sov,
ma na - im va - tov!
f

My Dreidel

Music by Samuel Goldfarb
Lyrics by Samuel S. Grossman
Arranged by Carol Matz

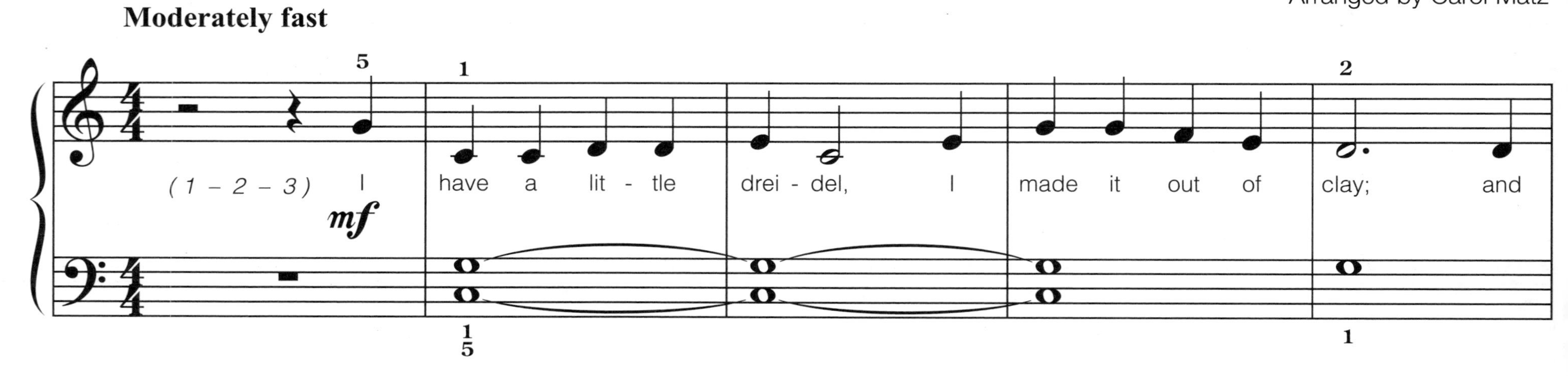

DUET PART (Student plays one octave higher)

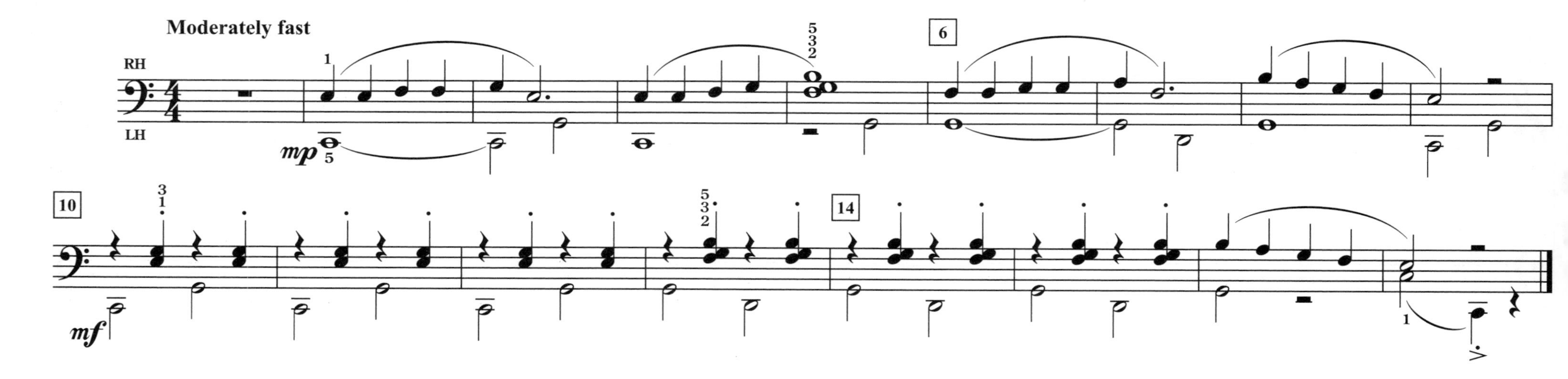

6
2
5
1
3
when it's dry and
read - y then
drei - del I shall
play. Oh,
f
1
5
10
5
2
drei - del, drei - del,
drei - del, I
made it out of
clay; and
1
5
1
14
4
5
1
when it's dry and
read - y then
drei - del I shall
play!
1
1
5

Dayeinu

Traditional
Arranged by Carol Matz

DUET PART (Student plays one octave higher)

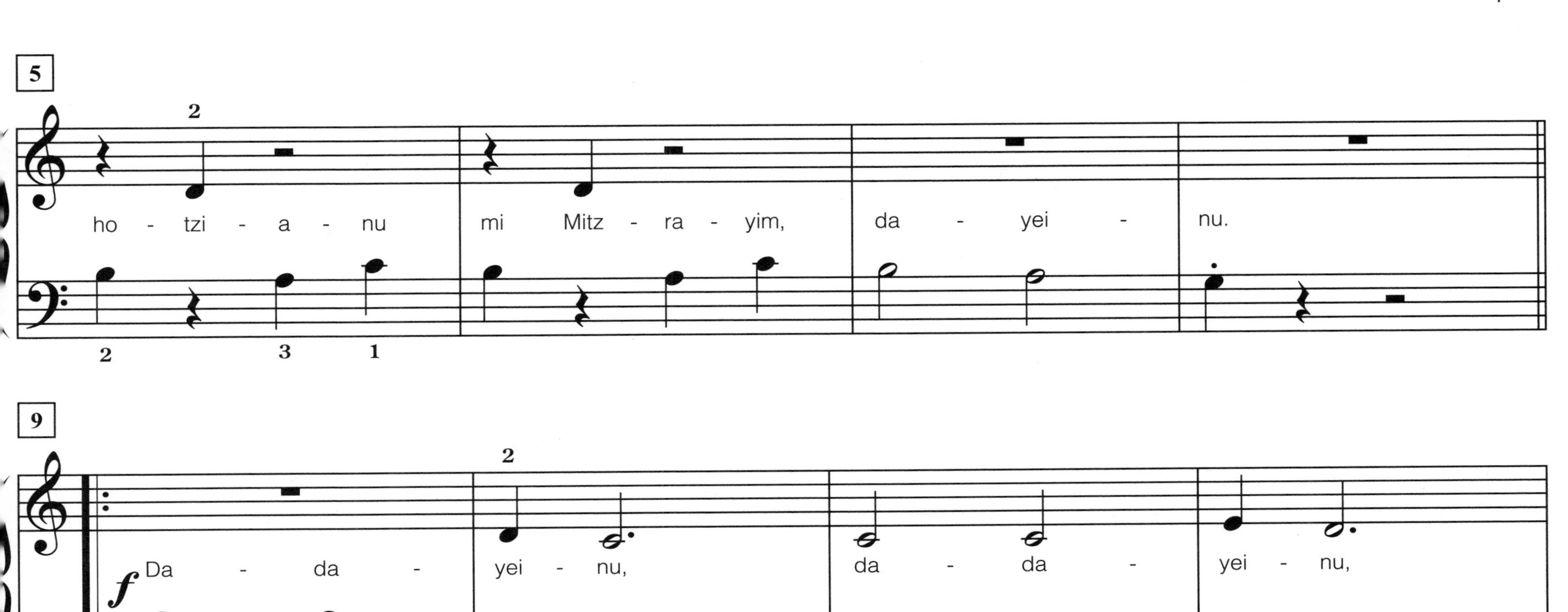
5
ho - tzi - a - nu
mi Mitz - ra - yim,
da - yei - nu.
9
Da - da - yei - nu,
da - da - yei - nu,

13
(repeat)
da - da - yei - nu, da - yei - nu, da - yei - nu.

Chag Purim

Traditional
Arranged by Carol Matz

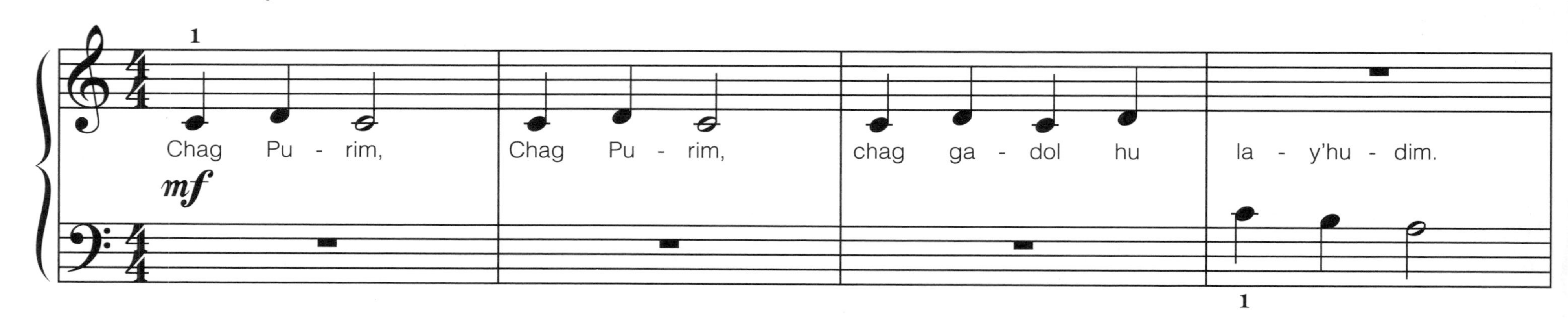

DUET PART (Student plays one octave higher)

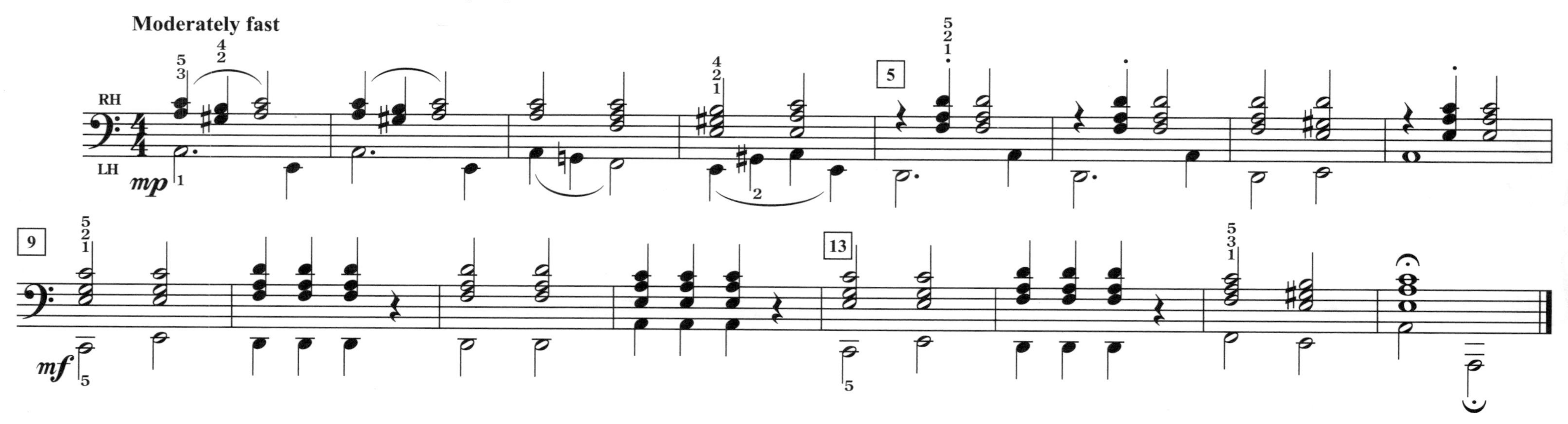

5
2
Ma - sei - chot,
ra - sha - nim
z'mi - rot ri - ku
dim.
3
1
9
3
Ha - va na - ri - sha
rash rash rash,
ha - va na - ri - sha
rash rash rash,
f
3
13
3
ha - va na - ri - sha
rash rash rash,
ba - ra - a - sha - nim.
3

Shabbat Candle Blessing

Traditional
Arranged by Carol Matz

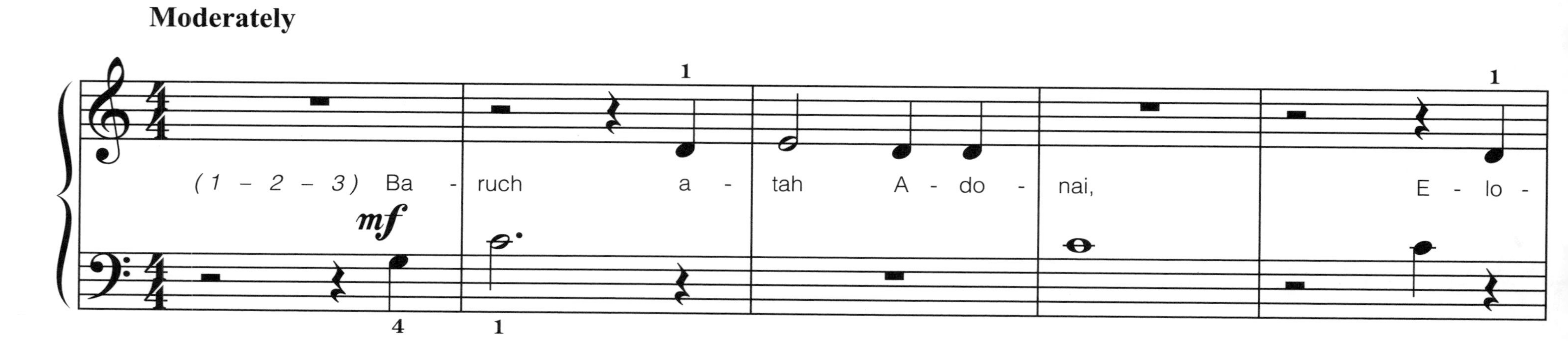

DUET PART (Student plays one octave higher)

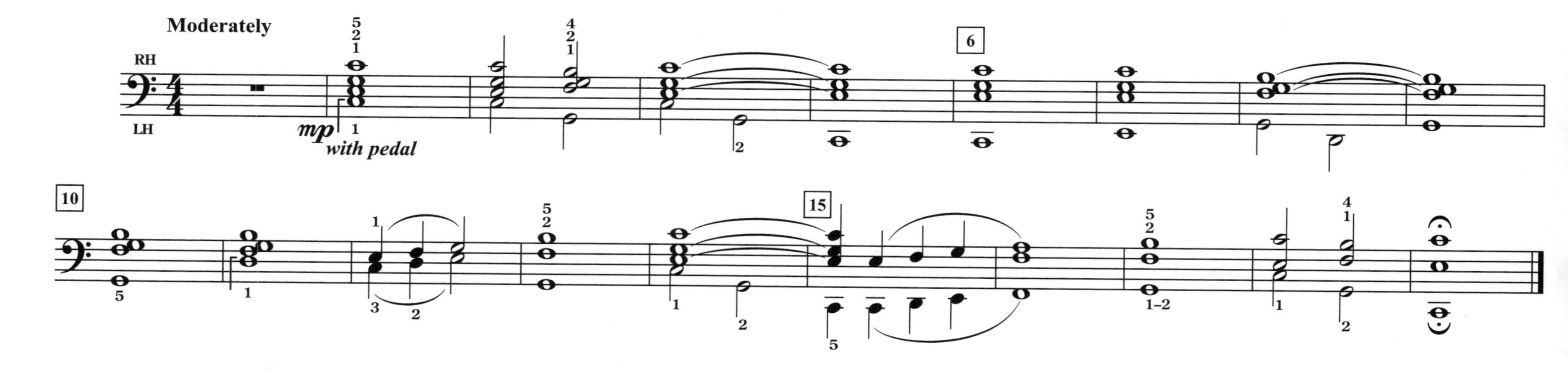

6
2
hei - nu
me - lech ha - o - lam,
a -
4
10
3
sher ki - d'
sha - nu b' -
mits vo
tav, v' - tsi -
va - nu
1
15
2
l' - had - lik
ner
shel
1
Shab -
bat.
1

Hinei Ma Tov

Traditional Folk Song
Words from Psalm 133
Arranged by Carol Matz

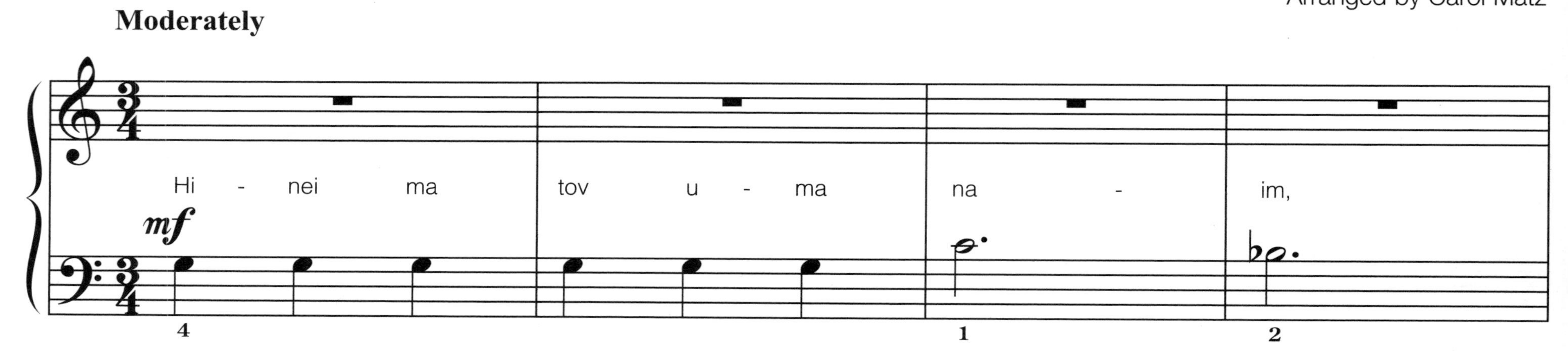

DUET PART (Student plays one octave higher)

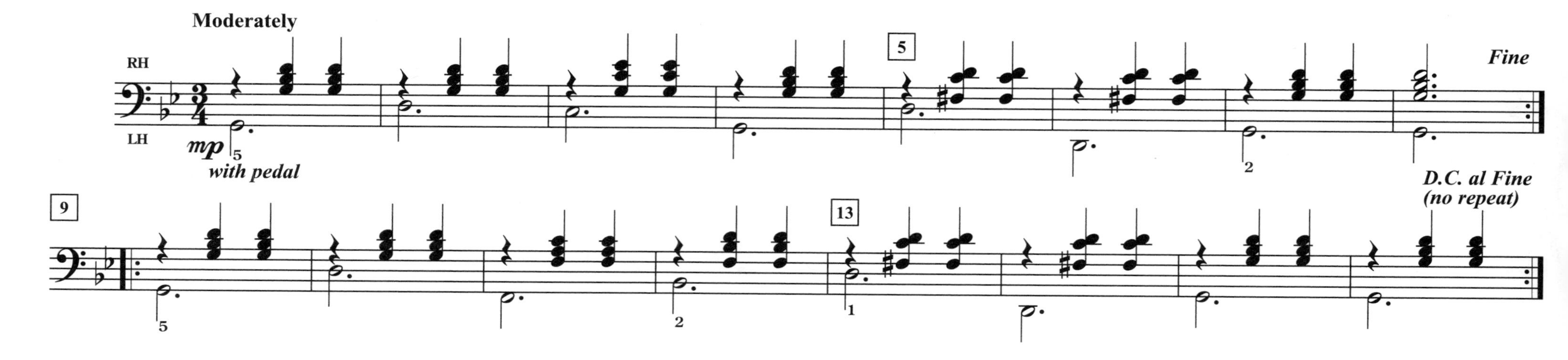

5
(repeat)
she - vet a - chim gam ya - chad.
3
9
2
5
3
Hi - nei ma tov
f

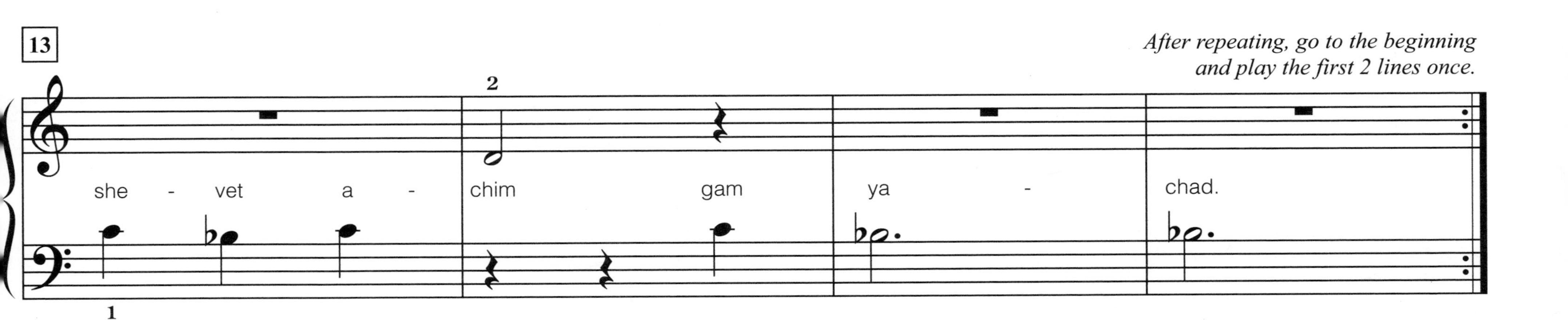
13
After repeating, go to the beginning
and play the first 2 lines once.
2
she - vet a - chim gam ya - chad.
1

Hatikva
(National Anthem of Israel)

Traditional Folk Tune
Words by Naftali Herz Imber
Arranged by Carol Matz

DUET PART (Student plays one octave higher)

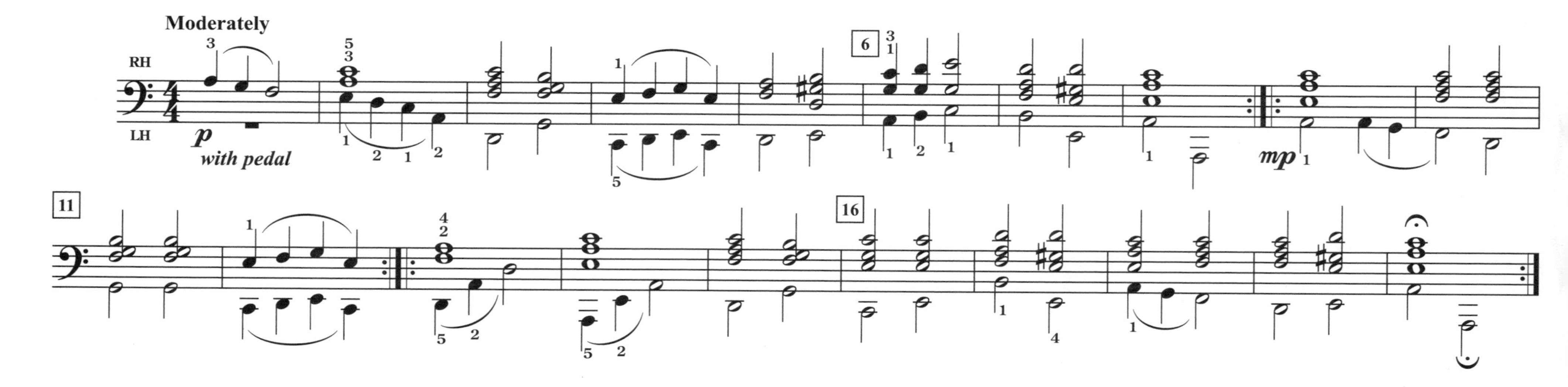

6
5
hu - di
Tzi - yon
ho - mi -
tzo - fi -
ya.
ya.
Od lo av - da
Ha - tik - va
mf
1
3
11
1
tik - va - tei - nu,
sh'not al pa - yim.
Li - yot am chof shi b' - ar -
1
16
2
tzei - nu e - retz Tzi - yon v'Ye - ru - sha - la - yim.
1

Go Down, Moses

Traditional Folk Song
Arranged by Carol Matz

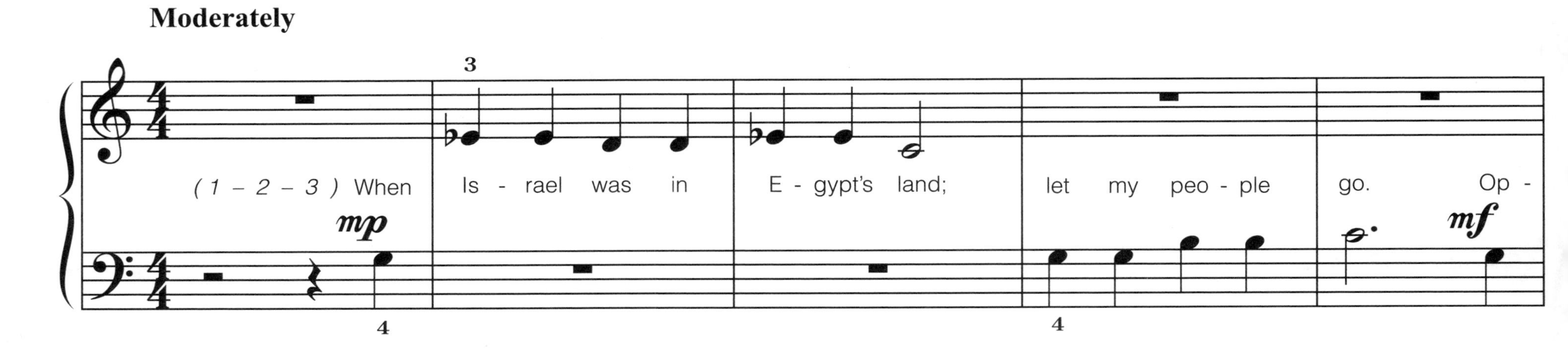

DUET PART (Student plays one octave higher)

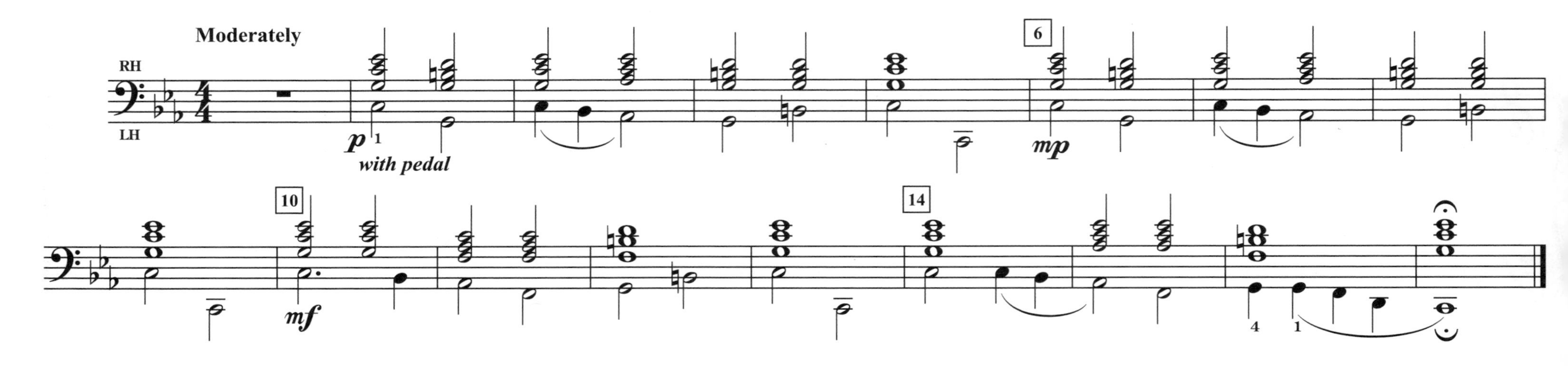

6
3
pressed so hard they
could not stand.
Let my peo - ple
go.
4
10
4
3
Go down
Mo - ses,
way down in
E - gypt's land.
f
1

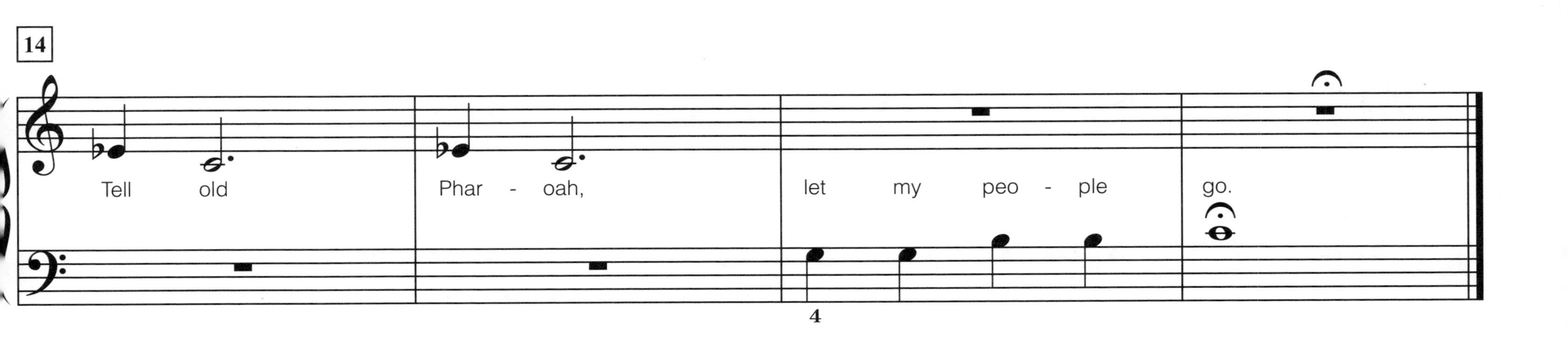
14
Tell old
Phar - oah,
let my peo - ple
go.
4

Siman Tov

Yiddish Folk Song
Arranged by Carol Matz

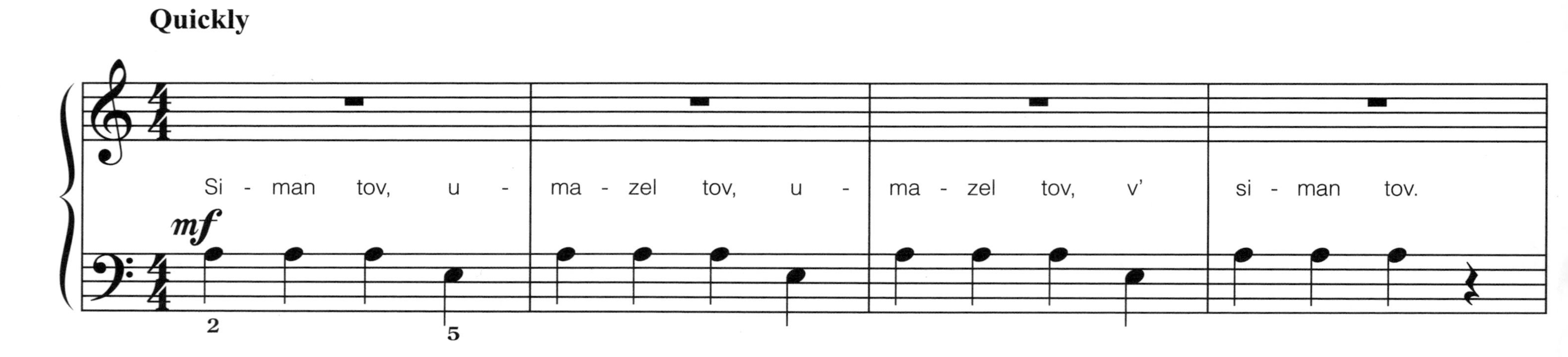

DUET PART (Student plays one octave higher)

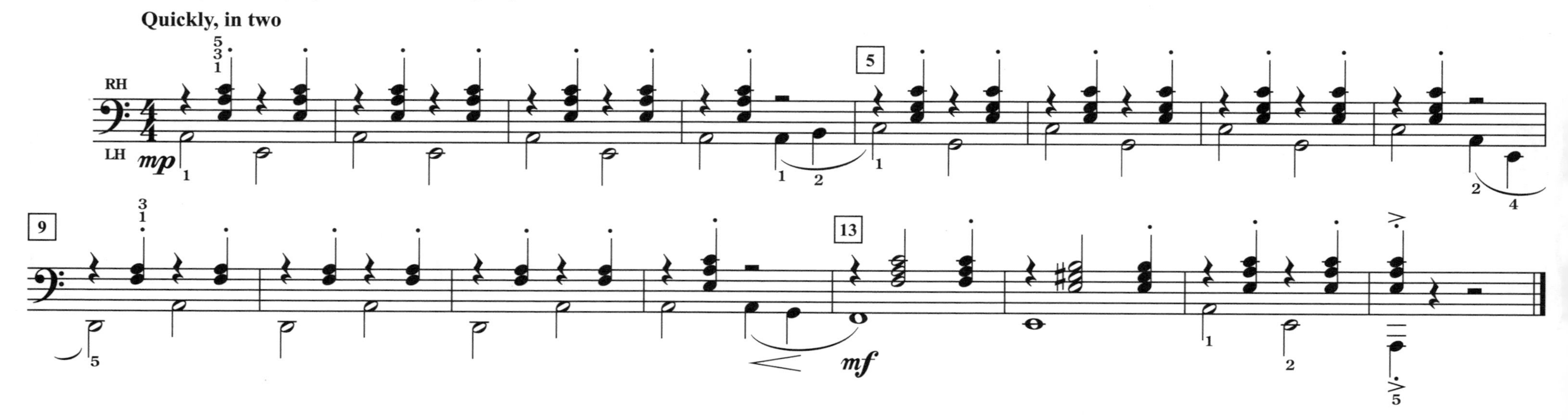

5
1
Si - man tov, u - ma - zel tov, u - ma - zel tov, v' si - man tov.
3
9
2
Si - man tov, u - ma - zel tov, u - ma - zel tov, v' si - man tov,
1
13
2
y' - hei la - nu.
f
1

Ein Keloheinu

Traditional
Arranged by Carol Matz

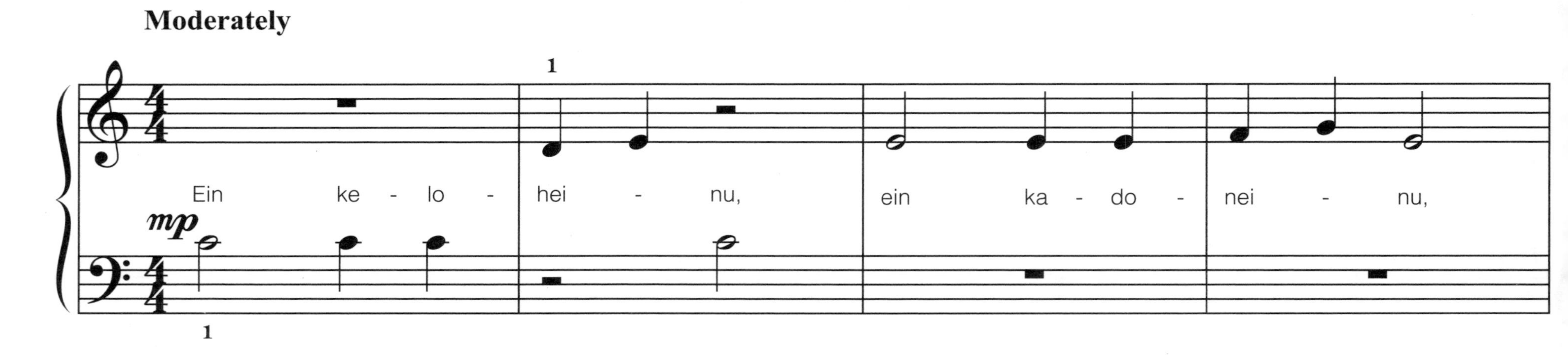

DUET PART (Student plays one octave higher)

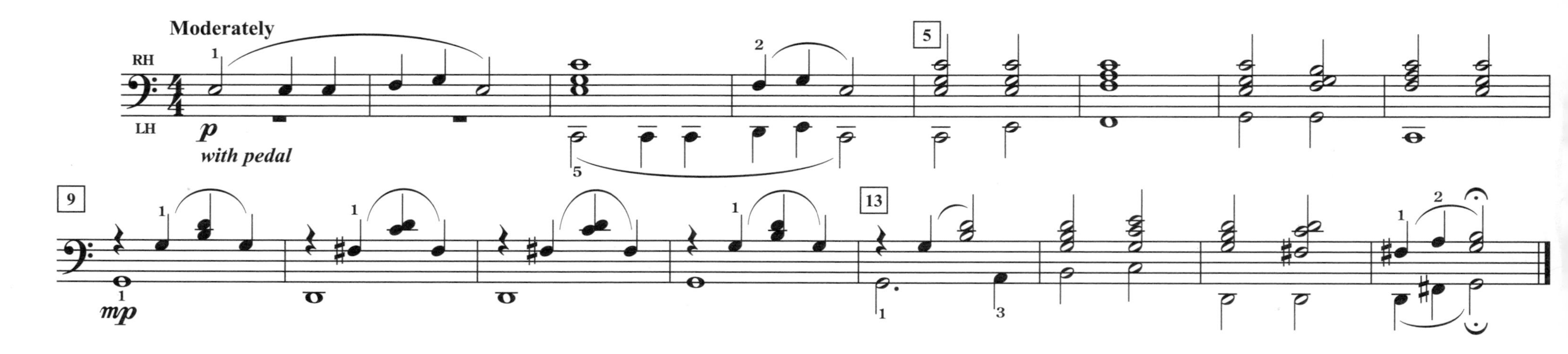

5
ein ke - mal - kei - nu, ein ke - mo - shi - ei - nu.
9
Mi ke - lo - hei - nu, mi cha - do - nei - nu,
mf
13
mi che - mal - kei - nu, mi che - mo - shi - ei - nu?
(move)

Heveinu Shalom Aleichem

Traditional Folk Song
Arranged by Carol Matz

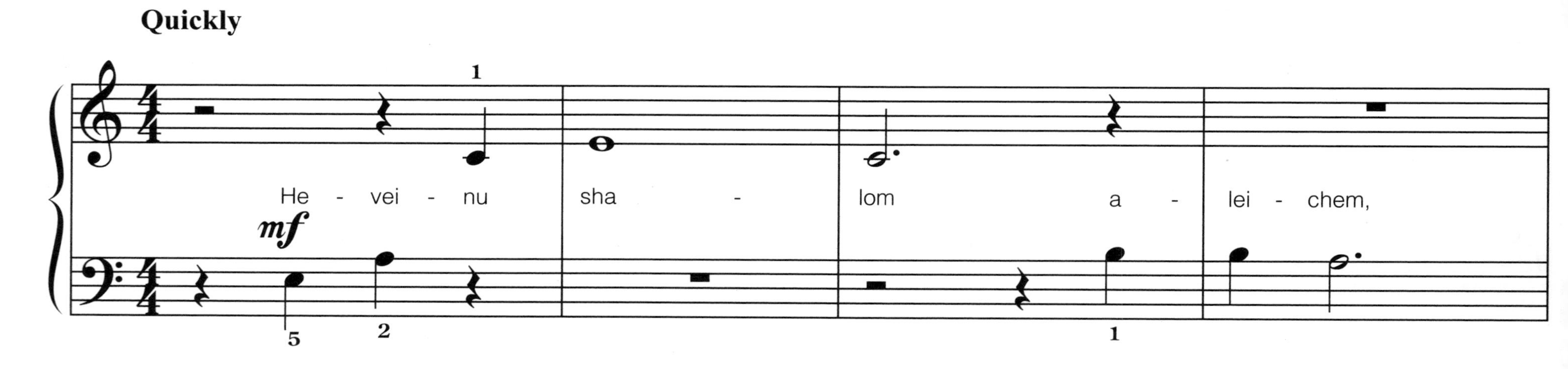

DUET PART (Student plays one octave higher)

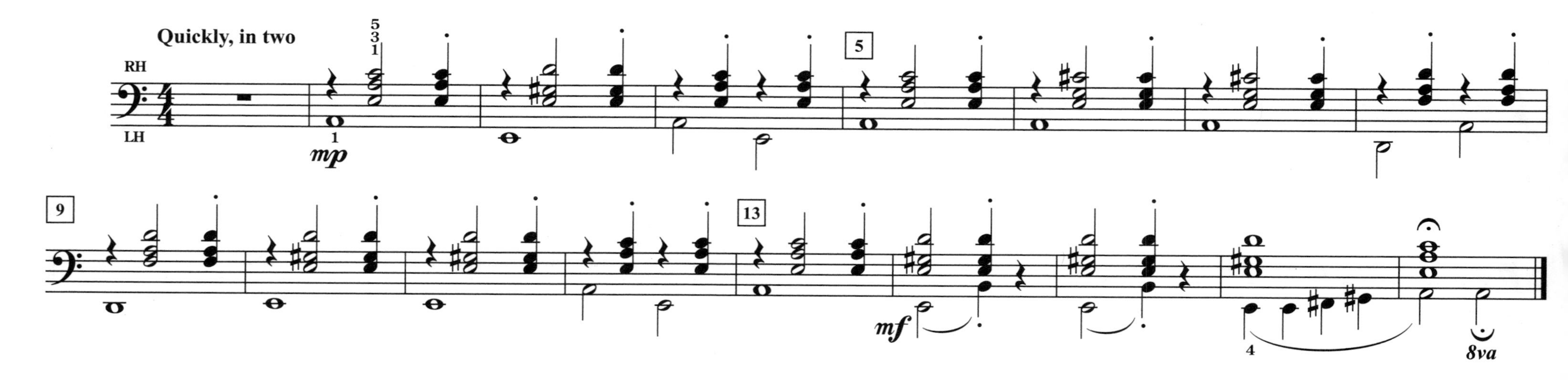

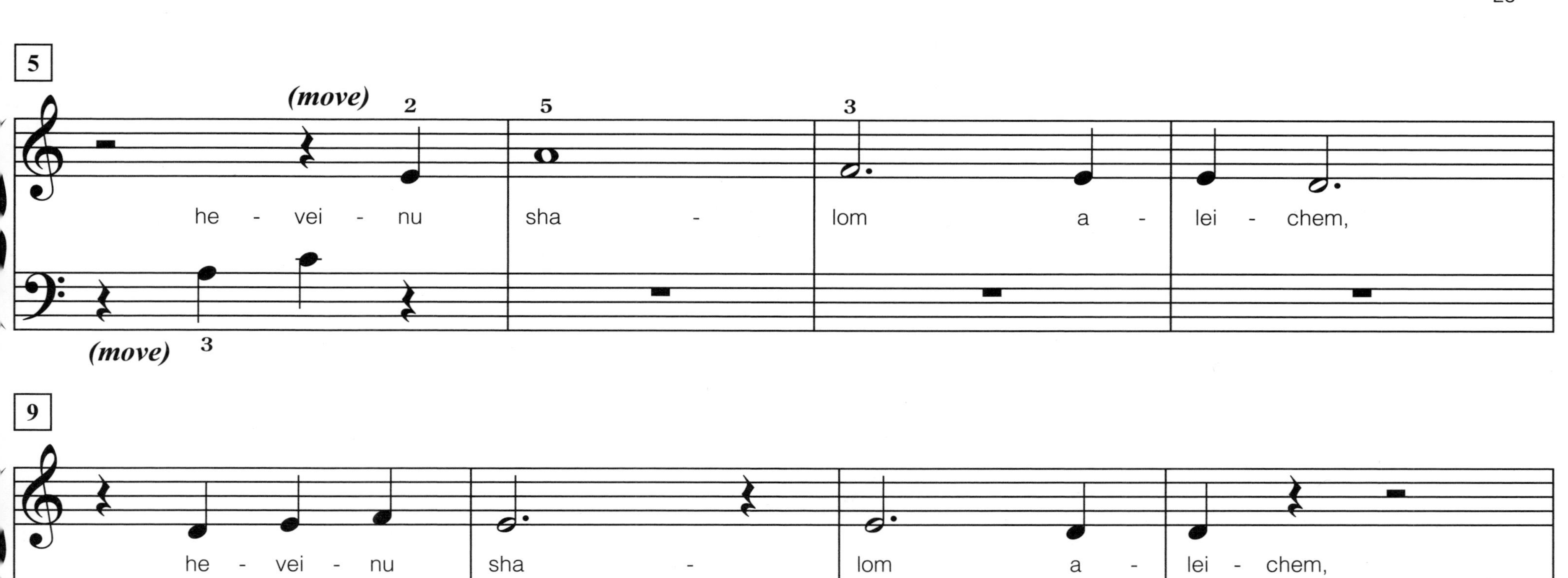
5
(move)
2
5
3
he - vei - nu
sha -
lom a -
lei - chem,
(move)
3
9
he - vei - nu
sha -
lom a -
lei - chem,
2
1

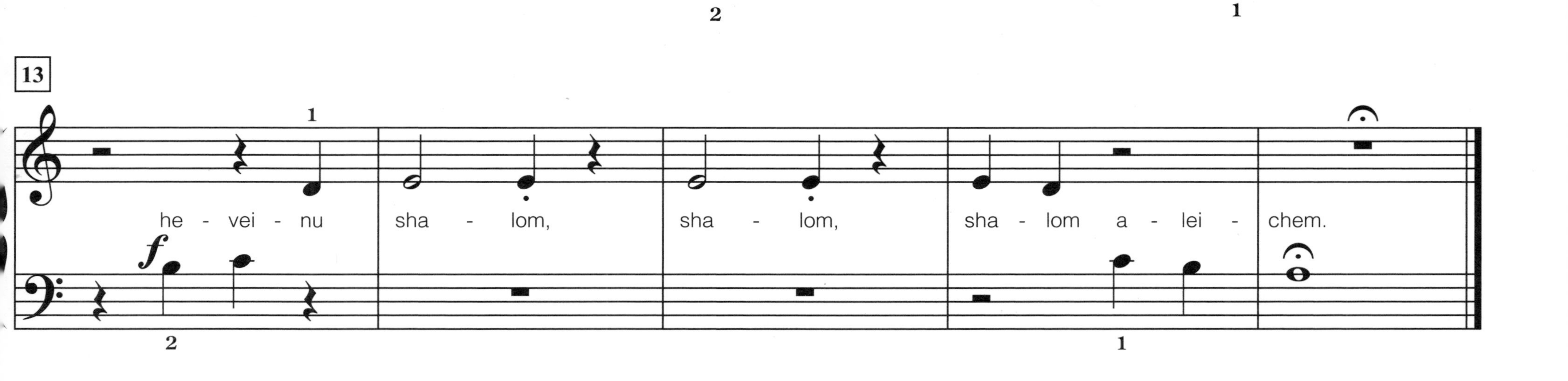
13
1
he - vei - nu
sha - lom,
sha - lom,
sha - lom a - lei -
chem.
f
2
1